DONNA R. RUTHERFORD

Heart Strings

THROUGH MY EYES

Poetic Fragrances
From My Heart

Heart Strings – Through My Eyes
Poetic Fragrances From My Heart

Poetic Fragrances in this book were written from 1998-2017

Printed in the United States of America

First Printing, 2018

ISBN: 978-0-9997807-2-5

Publishers:
Above The Line Press
McKinney, TX
www.abovethelinepress.com

"Like music, sometimes words
can't describe how you feel
You must feel it for yourself
You must experience it
Poetry has helped me
to inspire,
be compassionate, and
paint the words.

With each stroke of the pen I am
learning to breathe, to love, and
to live the lyrics my
heart composes."

~Donna R. Rutherford

DEDICATION

To my Lord and Savior Jesus Christ ... Thank You.
You continue to amaze me. You are the love song I
will forever sing.

ACKNOWLEDGEMENTS

To my family and friends, thank you for your
encouragement, prayers, love and support.

A special acknowledgement to my sister, Brenda.
You are such a joy in my life. Your encouragement
and love has helped me to continue to reach beyond
the horizon.

CONTENTS

Preface

I pray that the Lord Jesus Christ will bless the work of my hands by using these poetic fragrances to minister to your heart and spirit, as He reveals to you it's time for you to grow and shine.

The poetic fragrances were birthed from my devotional time with the Lord, and as He placed them in my spirit to share from my personal experience. Some of them can be bitter, sweet, or even whimsical.

A Mother's Wish

Slow down little girl
Slow down
There were days of skates and sun
Throwing the ball
Songs were sung

It was easy going around the block
Ringing that door bell
It's time to play
Come on out

Bikes, wagons, dolls, here we come
You got those jacks?
Oh Yeah! And some

Slow down little girl
Slow down
Where did you go?
Who is this over there?
I'm watching time slip you away
Stay little girl
Stay

Above The Storm

My God is right there!
He is in the midst of our storms taking us
to the other side

We may not like the storm
We may not even understand the storm

There are some storms the enemy brings
There are some storms from God
And at times, it can be hard to decipher between
the two

Even so, no matter what the day may bring,
KEEP PRAISING GOD!

Adjust Your Lens

Sometimes you need to have some quiet time just to reflect. Shut out the noise. The distractions. The negative vibes. And yes, in some cases, even people. Separating yourself from certain people may be required for a season. Do whatever is necessary to recapture your peace of mind, and get back on track

Reflecting allows you to see things in a different light. You're able to see more clearly. Your lens aren't as cloudy. You're able to see both sides of the situation. It's easy to see the full picture. It's just like wearing glasses. Adjustments need to be made to help you see better

For some people, their relationships have been damaged, and they realize they were putting more emphasis on the small issues that didn't really matter. Now they live with regrets because they can't undo the repercussions

It's so important to have a confidant that can view your issues from a different perspective. Godly counsel can also be an avenue of choice

Whether it's family or friends, know when it's time to pursue reconciliation, and when it's time to let go, walk away, and move on

Adversity

Don't let ADVERSITY cause you to become
BITTER

Disappointment, struggles, pain, etc. We all
experience it. It's called life

If you are bitter, you must kill it at the root

Be FREE!

Alone Or Lonely?

There is a big difference between being alone and
lonely. Which one are you?

Be honest with yourself. Be honest with God.
There's no shame in that. It's time to be real

Make your request known to the Lord. Wait on Him
for the answer. Allow the Lord to guide you along
your singleness journey

Bait & Switch

It looks pretty good
I like what I see
Is this the one?
I don't know, it could be

A lot to think about
Much to consider
I need to talk it over
I'll get back with ya

Don't miss this moment
What you need is right here
Sign on the dotted line
I'll make your troubles disappear

I didn't listen
Just didn't care
I silenced that still, small voice whispering in my ear

I took the bait
I should have known better
Didn't seek good counsel
I put myself in this dilemma

If I had to do it over
I would take a different route
Casting all my cares on the Lord
Trusting Him to work things out

Be Kind!

Be kind! Behind every person is a story. It doesn't matter what our background may be, we all have a few things in common. The need to be loved, respected, and valued is universal

We all experience difficulties and setbacks periodically. And it's not necessarily any fault of our own. It's called life. Stuff happens. But we know that it's only God's grace that keeps us daily

A kind word, offered prayer, a hug, or even a listening ear, are all acts of kindness that will minister to a person's spirit as they face life's challenges

So be kind!

Beyond The Job

Good morning Monday
Here we go again
On my way
Don't know what's in store today
Look beyond the JOB

Oh, I hate this traffic
Here comes grumpy
Sorry Lord
What does he want now?
Can I talk to you?
Do you have to?
Oops. Sorry again Lord
Please
God, why am I here?
Look beyond the JOB

I see something different in you
There's something special about you
What's wrong?
Look beyond the JOB

I trust you
Confidant
I have to tell you something
Pray for me
Wasn't expecting this
Look beyond the JOB

Can I Talk To You?

Hello
Can I talk to you?
One second
Give me a minute
What's up?
Well …
Wait. Hold on
Sorry about that
Now what?
This phone keeps ringing!
As you were saying
I was trying to say …
This is ridiculous!
Everything is happening now!
Whew
How can I help you?
Well, if you're too busy
What?
I'm never too busy for you
Now what were you saying?
I've been having these thoughts
What do you mean?
Oh, I forgot to email this
Can you wait a minute?
Don't go anywhere
I see you're busy
Who me?
Nah. This is normal for me
I do apologize
What's on your mind?

Nothing
It wasn't important
Okay
Have a good day
Did you hear what happened?
No. What's going on?
That guy you were talking to yesterday took his life
last night
He was struggling with depression
I guess he just needed someone to talk to

Change Your View

When you get up in the morning
What is the first thing you do?
What is your thought pattern?
So much to do
Not enough help
Not enough hours in the day
Lacking resources
Need financial help
Dread working on this project
Back is against the wall
The pressure is on
I can't do this
STOP! STOP! STOP!
Rewrite your story
Relax
Take another look
Change your view
Change your mindset
Shut out the noise
Pray
Talk to the Lord Jesus Christ
Give the Lord your fears
Give the Lord your concerns
Surround yourself with people who care
Reflect on God's goodness
Change your view

Come Now!

Don't wait until the mood hits you
Don't wait until the rain is gone
Don't wait until you got the right shoes
Don't wait until your makeup is on
Don't wait until you got the right clothes
Don't wait until your hairdo is dope
Don't wait until you hear the right song
Don't wait until your friends come along
Don't wait until you get the invite
Don't wait until you get things right
Don't wait until you get the phone call
Don't wait until you see the writing on the wall

The Day of Salvation is here

Come Now!

Dancing In My Joy!

I arise
I arise
My hands lifted high
With a song in my heart
A praise in my mouth
Here I am Lord
I'm dancing in my Joy!

I've given you my fears
In exchange for your peace
Moving forward in your grace
Trusting you Jesus all the way
Here I am Lord
I'm dancing in my Joy!

Your presence is so sweet
I will never be the same
You are my hope and strength
To face each day
Here I am Lord
I'm dancing in my Joy!

Dear Lord

My Lord, how glorious is Your Name
How wonderful your works
Your love is beyond comprehension
Awesome are your ways
The Name of Jesus forever I will proclaim

When I think about your goodness
I know I am never alone
You cause me to smile every day
You are the one I run to
Strong tower in times of trouble
You are my Rock
My strength
My joy
The lifter of my head

You cause me to sing
I will sing with joy
Forever I will speak Your Name

Do You Love Me

Now?

Good morning, Lord!
I got up early and prayed one hour
I don't usually pray that long

I cooked a meal today for a friend of mine
Oh, last week I helped a single mother out with some
clothes for her three children
Tomorrow I'll be helping some people who are
homeless
I took the time to minister to someone yesterday
about salvation
I'm trying to think about anything else I can do that
would meet your approval
There's got to be more things I can do that would
make you love me
It's not that I don't believe you do
I just want to feel secure that I'm okay with You
I'm not trying to get any brownie points or anything

REALLY? Well, it sure sounds like it

I wonder how many of us have subconsciously
wondered if we must earn the love of God
We think God has some imaginary measuring stick
He uses against us

Man may think we don't measure up to their standard
But God isn't like that
He's not like man
And I'm so glad about it!

To understand just how much God loves us, we need
to be strengthened on the inside by the Holy Spirit
We need to be rooted and grounded in love
It's through our personal, intimate relationship with
Jesus Christ that we discover who we are in Him,
what we mean to Him, and what He was willing to do
for us
The Holy Spirit continues to reveal Christ to us as we
study the Word of God

Jesus Christ laid down His life for us willingly
He loved us from the foundation of the world
He loved us while we were still in our mother's womb
He loves us while we were still in our sins

He pursued us
He went after us
He wooed us
He tugged at our heart
He found us

And when we finally surrendered, the love affair
began
Our love affair with Jesus Christ is eternal
He did everything for us on the Cross at Calvary

Now get it through your head
Settle it in your spirit
There is NOTHING you must do to earn God's love

God loves us freely
He gave us eternal life
That should be proof enough

Enough Said

Sometimes you see people for who they really are

Forgive and love them anyway

and

KEEP IT MOVING!

Evolve

Evolve into the best YOU that you can be

The process of discovering YOU is ever evolving

There's a lot to learn about yourself

Know your worth

Your journey can be beautiful

Expose It

Don't expect the wound to heal if you don't remove
the bandage and expose it

If you want to be healed
stop covering up the wound

Forgive Anyway

Forgive anyway
Your soul depends on it
A choice to forgive someone is in your hands now
It's either 'YES I WILL' or 'NO I WON'T'
You must decide
You can't say, "I'll think about it"
"I'll do it later"
Tomorrow isn't promised to anyone
Your next breath isn't promised to you
Forgive and ask the Lord to bring the healing
If you're wounded or hurt in your spirit, only God
can heal that
Not that person who hurt you

Forgiving someone is tied to your relationship with
Father God, make it right
You can still take the time to talk to that person who
hurt you
Choose to forgive, and trust the Lord to heal

Every day we are faced with decisions and choices
that affect our lives
Some may be more serious than others
Forgiveness would fall into the eternity category
Whatever you do, you don't want to wait on this one
Forgiveness is not based on your feelings
It's what you decide to do
And if you need help to forgive, just be honest and
ask God to help you, He will

Get Off The Throne ...

It Belongs To God

I can't believe I've done all these great things!
Did you see the standing ovation I received?
So many people congratulated me after the event
I received a bunch of phone calls
Too many to count
I'm already making plans for the next project
I guess I need a team
On second thought, I can do it all myself
At least I know I'm reliable, can you believe it?
I'm already getting followers on social media
Need to go shopping for my speaking engagement
Haven't received that phone call yet
I know I will
They'd be stupid to pass me up
I got so many ideas
I guess I can take credit for the recognition
Those other guys didn't do too much
I did most of the hard work
I wonder how far up the ladder I can go
Wouldn't hurt to try
I'll do whatever it takes
Any company would be blessed to have me on staff
I can shake things up
Get those employees in line, I'll be in charge for sure
I need to get recognized on the radio and TV

Maybe I should submit an article in the newspaper
Hollywood here I come!

Give Yourself

Permission

Give yourself permission

To fail
To forgive
To heal
To grow

Whatever it takes for you to feel good about yourself again, to be made whole, to love YOU, take the first step towards getting your power back

God Got Your Back!

New Day
New Week
New Battles
New Territories
New Victories
New Mercies
New Strength

We are more than a conqueror!
Stand firm in it
Walk in it
Talk like it
Live like it

God Got Your Back!

God Is My Guide

My path is clear when I let God be my guide

No stress or trying to figure things out

No worrying over how things are going to work out

There's peace and rest in trusting that my life is in the
Lord's hands

He has already ordered my steps

While on this journey, He is the best guide there is

God's Love Letter

Everything you need is right here

The Bible

The Word of God

A love story from God Himself written to us

Go beyond just reading the pages of the Bible, to a personal relationship

Get to know the Author

Don't just read about Him

Whatever it is you're looking for is right here

Everything you need is right here

Heart Check

Lord Jesus Christ
Create in me a clean heart

We all need a daily examination of our spiritual heart
It's important that we are physically healthy
But we can't neglect the more weightier matters of life
The Holy Spirit is looking at our heart
If we ask Him, He's faithful to clean out anything that
is not pleasing to Him

Highest Praise

Hallelujah! Almighty God
Children of God
Let your voice ring
We sing Glory to the Holy One
We give you the Highest Praise
We worship you Heavenly Father
We praise you from our hearts
We come before your gates with Thanksgiving
As we enter your courts with Praise
Let Your Glory fill this place
Holy hands to you we raise
You are our God
Lord, we magnify You
We glorify You
We bless your Holy Name
Let everything that hath breath give you the Highest
Praise

How Beautiful!

O Lord Jesus Christ, how beautiful you are!
Your glory and splendor is forevermore
All power and authority is in Your Name
The Name above all names

How Majestic!
How Glorious!
How Beautiful!

A thousand tongues are never enough to give you
praise
To speak your Wonder
Amazing are you God!
Heaven and earth declare your beauty

How Majestic!
How Glorious!
How Beautiful!

How Long?

Another day
It starts the same
Nothing to look forward to
I must face it
Don't want to face it
The writing is on the wall
I'm tired
How long?
Open your eyes
Wake Up!

Given yourself over, and over, again
Just a shoulder to cry on
Your account is empty
Nothing in return
Life slipping away
Years wasted
Fear is here
How long?
Open your eyes
Wake Up!

He's not that way
Or is he?
He just needs more time
I've invested so much
Unappreciative
Anger takes root
Fight!
How long?

Open your eyes
Wake Up!

Confront him
Suspicious ways
Just waiting around
Don't have time for you
Actions speak louder than words
Why do I put up with this foolishness?
In search of ME
How long?
Open your eyes
Wake Up!

I Belong To You

I know who I belong to
It's wonderful when you finally realize who you are
You're not a threat to the enemy until that happens

My Father God is the King of Kings
And the Lord of Lords

I'm the apple of His eye

I Didn't See You

Every now and then
You would call
Laugh a little
Joke a little
Small talk
Stuff to do
I didn't see you

Lunchtime
Movie time
Let's get it in
Promises made
We can try again

Something happened
The space in between became more
You're still going through
I didn't see you

I apologize
I wasn't there
Should have put forth more effort
It's time to clear the air

Where do I start?
I want to make amends
Whatever it takes
I miss you, my friend

I Know Who Can

I can't fix it
But I know who can

I can't heal it
But I know who can

I can't take away the pain
But I know who can

I can't change it
But I know who can

I can't make you whole
But I know who can

I can't make you happy
But I know who can

I can't give you joy
But I know who can

I can't give life
But I know who can

LET'S TALK!

I Love You Both The Same

Gotta get to work
The clock is ticking
You got everything?
Yeah
Wait. My keys
One more thing
A kiss for the little ones
There ya go
Lord, bless them
Okay. I'm off
Errands to run
Come on
You better behave yourself
Wait until your father gets home
I didn't do anything!
It was her fault
Dinnertime
Go wash your hands
Keys in the door
DADDY'S HOME!
Running
Daddy! Daddy! Daddy!
There's my little ones!
Pick me up daddy!
I was here first
No. Pick me up!

No fighting girls
I love you both the same
Come on, calm down
How was your day?
I brought you something home
Yay!
Let me see
Hear ya go
How come she got that one?
I want that one!
Wait a minute, girls
You both received the same thing
Just a different color
Crying!
Why are you crying?
You love her more!
Why would you say that?
Still crying!
Because
Because what?
Don't I treat you the same?
Don't I show my love to you both?
Don't I go out of my way to help you?
Don't you know how much I love you?
You are both my children
I love you both the same
You don't have to fight for my attention
You don't have to fight for my affection
Don't be mad at your sister
Don't be jealous of your sister
I have no favorites
Always remember
I love you both the same

I pray that is an ah-hah moment for you.
There are no favorites in the Kingdom of God.
God loves us all the same

I See Blue

I see it
It's within my reach
I can have it
I deserve it
I'm worthy to receive it

Every morning
When I rise
I ask myself that question
You know, that question

It's always there
Lingering
Hovering
Listening
Waiting to hear from me

I won't make a move until you do
I'm waiting on you
Just waiting on you

When you're ready
Just let me know
Take another look
Come one, one more look

Now looking beyond what I know
You've given me strength to reach my goal
I no longer ask why
I say, why not?

I'm looking above
I see blue
Lord, you've given me eyes to see
My hope is in you

I See Double

One day you're cheering your friend on
The next day you're telling them it won't work

One day you're packing Thanksgiving baskets for
your church
The next day you're telling a homeless person
to get a job

One day you're sobbing tears with a coworker
The next day you're gossiping about them in the
ladies' restroom

One day you're praying with someone who trusts you
as a confidant
The next day you're sharing their information
with your crew

One day you're on social media talking about
health concerns
The next day you're in the store buying a
box of cigarettes

One day you're putting your son out of your house
because of one mistake
The next day you're talking to your neighbor's son
about second chances

One day you're talking to someone about their
obesity

The next day you take two trips to a fast-food
restaurant

One day you have an argument with your mother, and
hang up on the phone
The next day you're talking to a stranger about the
importance of forgiveness

I see double

I Want To Be

Be Compassionate
Be Courageous
Be Solemn
Be Bold
Be Unique
Be Authentic
Be Zippy
Be Respectful
Be Unselfish
Be Teachable
Be Zealous
Be Steadfast
Be Hopeful
Be Tenacious
Be Unshakable
Be Gracious
Be Fruitful
Be Trustworthy
Be Confident
Be Hospitable
Be Unstoppable
Be Truthful

Be Essential
Be Enthused
Be Unwavering
Be Efficient
Be Pleasant
Be Persistent
Be Generous
Be Humble
Be Grateful
Be Kind
Be Sociable
Be Radiant
Be Valuable
Be Powerful
Be Forgiving
Be Loving
Be Admirable
Be Effective
Be Memorable
Be Reliable
Be Established
Be Successful

In The Presence Of

The King

Stripped of everything I think I am
Forgetting about my earthly possessions
Letting go of my rights I hold so dearly
Somehow trying to prove a point doesn't matter
Oh! The Glory of Your Presence!
Falling to my knees
In the presence of THE KING

Unclean!
Unclean!
My heart cries out for mercy
Who am I?
Tears streaming down my face
Seeking forgiveness in this Holy Place
Oh! The Glory of Your Presence!
Lifting trembling hands
In the presence of THE KING

Such a sweet aroma
I know you are near
Your peace surrounds me
Like I've never felt before
Oh! The Glory of Your Presence!
I've been changed
In the presence of THE KING

Invisible

Sunlight delight
Stiletto heels are right
Spring is here
Let the costumes begin

Precious stones
No one will ever know
I wore the same dress
Two weeks ago

Glimmer and glam
You make your choice
One thing for sure
You'll never be bored

Action
Stars
Lights
The day is finally here
For me to make my entrance
My name should be on this seat right here

Yellow
Purple
Pink
What should the color be?
It doesn't really matter
They'll never forget me

Is my hat big enough?

The feather is HOT!
Special effects are needed to make this moment POP!

All eyes are on me
O how grand
Fake friends are not real
O if looks could kill
But at least for today
I'm not invisible

It Didn't Destroy Me

Whatever the IT is
The lies
The backstabbing
The fear
The insecurities
The fake friends
The struggles
The hardships
The health issues
The personal loss
Through it all
My IT didn't destroy me

I don't know what your IT is
Only you know that
Determine in your mind and spirit
Whatever your IT is
You will not be destroyed
You shall live
You shall not die
You shall live to tell your story

Its Done

You don't have to take on the sins of the world

Someone else already did that

His name is Jesus Christ

The greatest gift we can give someone is directing
them to the one who bore our sins, sickness, diseases,
and gave us eternal life

His name is Jesus Christ

He did it all for us

It's Time To Fly

It's time to fly

Every pain

Every tear

Every hurt

Every disappointment

These were all used as stepping stones to your destiny
while on your journey

Your transformation will be the wind to help you
spread your wings and fly

It's Time To Shift!

There is only one way to go Baby … and that's UP!

Be encouraged
It's time for a change
God is doing great things
You are not forgotten
Get ready for the SHIFT!

Just B-r-e-a-t-h-e

It's here
Another day is here
Where's my list?
I need my list

So many things to do
So many places to go
Chile, don't worry
No need to make a fuss

I'm awake now
Why am I awake now?
The day is not over
What's the rush?

I can do it
I can do it all
Gotta get moving
Been down this road before

Slow down li'l Momma
God will see you through
Always remember where your strength comes from

To everyone in a hurry
Important things in your life are slipping away
Just B-R-E-A-T-H-E
Tomorrow is another day

Just Like A Child

Running outside
Playing around
Laughing and singing
Not a care in the world
Not thinking about tomorrow
Happy about today
Just like a child

My Mom and Daddy take care of me
They take care of my needs
I'm not worried
They promised me
I believe what they said
Just like a child

When I fall down
They pick me up
When I'm in trouble
They help me
When I mess up
They still love me
I look to them to make everything alright
Just like a child

Let It Rain

Holy Lord send the rain
Rain down on us
Pour out your abundance of rain
We cry out
Right now
Right now
Let it rain
Dear Jesus
Let it rain

Shower us Lord with your blessings
Rain on us mighty God with your provisions
Bless the work of our hands
You have given us the land
Let it rain
Heavenly Father
Our provider
Open your flood gates
Let it rain

Let Me Cry Through

You

Thinking about you
The pain is deep
Words cannot explain how I feel
The grief is real
Questions are still around
Yes, they hang around
For how long I do not know
But you are real
I know you are real
When in despair you are real
"Go On" you tell me
And try I do
Every day is a new day
Let me cry through you

The tears still come
The ache is still there
"I know" you tell me, I will be there still
"Go On" you tell me
Let me cry through you

Each day you take me
The journey is real
Through it all, I will be there still
Peace has come
I've opened the door

I hear your voice saying once more
"Go On" you tell me
Let me cry through you

Let The Healing Begin

Truth can hurt
But it needs to be spoken
It needs to be heard
It needs to be received
It can be so painful
It can also be freeing

Speak from your heart
Ask for ears to really hear
Be real without judging
Let the healing begin

Lift Your Head

Lift your head all ye saints!
Why are you cast down?
Why is your countenance sorrowful?
Our God is great!
Our God is mighty!
Lift your head all ye saints!

His throne is everlasting
His mercy endures forever
Fall on your knees and bless His Holy Name!
Sing praises to our God
Let His goodness be known throughout the earth
Lift your head all ye saints!

Love On Display

Put the love of Jesus Christ on display

Let His love be SEEN

Let His love be FELT

Let His love be REMEMBERED

Love Your Neighbor

Off to the races we go
Wandering to and fro
Without a care
Without a concern
We live our lives as best we can

Take a walk
What do you see?
Love your neighbor
You ask of me

Every day we look
But do not see
The world is full
But lives are empty

Am I my brother's keeper?
Tell me, what do you think?
Someone prayed for you
Homage to our Lord Jesus Christ is due

Share my love
You are salt of the earth
Love your neighbor
Proclaiming God's Name through the world

Mercy

Mercy RECEIVED lives on
through Mercy GIVEN

Lord, your mercy endures forever
Help us to be mindful of this as we confront
situations that can be challenging in our walk with
You.

Mingle

How can you get to know someone if you don't
spend time with them?

Don't assume anything about someone

Get to know that person for yourself

Spend time with them

Allow them to get to know you

Mountain Be Gone!

Your mountain is trying to keep you
from
getting to the other side …

TELL IT TO MOVE!

Move On!

When are you going to stop holding someone
HOSTAGE because of their mistakes?
Forgive
Free them
Free yourself
Learn the lesson
MOVE ON!

When are you going to stop reminding people of their
faults?
Forgive
Stop pointing that finger
MOVE ON!

When are you going to be the solution instead of the
problem?
Forgive
Be a blessing to someone
MOVE ON!

My Cry

Thou O Lord, are my shield
In the morning, I cry to thee
I cry out, Mercy
I cry out, Mercy

In your face
Glory reigns
You are here in this place
Fill my heart Lord
Fill my heart Lord
With your grace

Everywhere I go
I see you
I see you
I see you

In Your Name
I find rest
You are my peace for weariness

Now I will sing
Yes, I will shout
My God lives
My God lives
He brought me out

My Joy!

How marvelous are you, O God!
There is no one like you
No one before you
No one after you
You rule and reign in all your Glory
I sing because of you
You are life forevermore
The keeper of my heart
My sustainer
My Joy!
My Joy!
My Joy!
All praise, honor, and glory belongs to you, O God!

My Prayer

Dear Heavenly Father
I pray for those whom You have given a voice that
needs to be heard
Give them the courage and strength to speak Your
truth as You lead
Help them to be an open vessel who can only be
filled by YOU
I ask this in Jesus Name
Amen

New Eyes

Let's get beyond the exterior of a person
Beyond the personality
Look beyond the color of their skin
See beyond their age
Try seeing beyond whether you think you have
anything in common with them

The Lord said we are to love one another, and know a
person by their spirit

We need to ask the Lord to give us new eyes, so we
can see one another as He does

When I look at you I should see a brother or sister in
Jesus Christ first

No Drama Zone

Don't receive drama and toxic people into your life
and spirit
That's foolish
Make room for love, happiness, peace and joy
Respect and love yourself
Set boundaries
Go where the love is
You deserve it

Not Right Now

Just one more minute
The clock is ticking
Make a move
I will
Not right now

I need more time
Decide
The calendar has room
I'll do it

Tomorrow has come
Today is the day
Just one more thing
One more call
Get it done
Not right now

Thought I heard a knock at the door
Answer the door
Salvation is here
I've heard you before
Can I come in?
Not right now

One Name

There's only ONE NAME
Above all names

JESUS CHRIST is that name

There's no other name above your struggles, pain,
sickness, diseases, and yes, even death

All power, honor, praise and glory belongs to this
name
JESUS CHRIST
He has conquered
Because he lives … you and I live

Only You, Lord

We need you Lord
We are loss without you
You alone are our hope and help in times of trouble
We cry out to you

Lord, we call upon Your Name for help
We humbly pray to you asking for your forgiveness,
and intervention in our lives
Make our hearts tender to hear from you
Only you can change the heart of man

Come Holy Spirit and make your presence known in
our midst
We need you

God, your mercy endures forever
You have always been so loving and kind to us,
despite our failing to recognize who You are, and our
need to have You in our lives

Please forgive us

Here we are

Over, And Over, Again

O Lord
I'm so at peace
You captured my heart
You know just when to make your presence known
It's sweet
The time with you is sweet
Whether I'm listening to music
Looking out the window
Or even quiet time in the middle of the night
Your presence is near
Over, and over, again

You cause me to smile
Even in the little things
Every moment with you matters
I hear the laughter in a child
It's you
A tear streaming down the face with words unspoken
It's you
A sparkle in eyes filled with joy
It's you
You give comfort
Over, and over, again

In the storm, you carry me
When I am weak
You hold me
When I am afraid
I run to you
When I am insecure

You assure me
Every morning I see you in the sunrise
You are my best friend
Over, and over, again

Praise The Lord

Praise the Name of Jesus
Praise His Name in all the earth

Praise Him in the heavens
Behold His mighty works

Praise the Lord!
Praise Him all ye people

Praise the Lord!
Shout with joy

Praise the Lord!
Praise Him from every nation

O come before Him
Let's worship and adore Him

Lift His Name with one voice
Praise the Lord!

Pray About It First

A PRAYER before ACTION is wisdom

Pray about it first before you decide to take matters
into your own hands

Emotions can run very high, especially in a heated
conversation

Once words are spoken, you can't take them back

The enemy is the author of confusion and conflict

Pray to the Lord for guidance and direction

Be patient while you wait for His answer

His truth will be revealed

Purpose Driven

Make it happen!

Everything you do counts!

Even the small things matter to reach your goal!

Real Talk

REAL TALK:
Are you jealous of someone? Are you envious of
what God is doing in their life? Do you find yourself
thinking more about what's happening to them,
instead of focusing on what God is doing in your life?
Do you think God is giving them favor, and has
forgotten about you? Do you cringe when you hear
their name? Do you find yourself avoiding being in
their presence? Do you follow them on social media
hoping to fit in their "village?" Do you look to them
for your "hook-ups?"

If you've answered YES to any of these questions,
then you have a heart issue. It's called jealous, envy,
covetous. That's right. It may be hard to swallow,
but it's the truth

Admit it. Be honest with yourself. Be honest with
God. I had to. It can be downright embarrassing to
admit it. It's worth it, though. The burden can be
lifted, and you can be set free. God knows your heart
anyway. You don't. The heart is deceitful. When the
Holy Spirit is tugging at your heart regarding this
issue, it's time to get it right. It's time to settle the
matter

It's time to STOP feeling jealous, envious, or coveting
what someone else has. God is not stingy in giving
His blessings and favor. He's no respect of persons.
He's a good Father that gives good gifts

Don't allow the enemy to steal your peace of mind and joy with thoughts that you don't have enough, you don't matter, or God doesn't really care about you

Don't believe the enemy's LIES

Remember Me

It's so important to remember the elderly, and
continue to pray for them
They have a special place in the heart of God and
society

We should always show them that they are not
forgotten, and that they still matter

Giving them honor and respect pleases the Lord

To the elderly I say …

You are not forgotten
You still matter
You have a place in my heart

Respect Yourself

Set your boundaries
Set your standards
Don't ignore the warning signs of abuse
Emotional abuse – Don't tolerate
Physical abuse – Don't tolerate
Forgiveness does not mean weakness
You're not dumping ground
Don't chase after people
You're not a doormat
Don't feed off drama
Don't make excuses for someone else disrespecting you
Don't lose yourself because of rejection
If people are interested in your business, they will support it
Actions speak louder than words
Don't try and be a copycat
There's only one YOU
Love and respect yourself enough to not tolerate disrespect from anyone

Respect Yourself

Seasons

Lord, in every season I go through,
please help me to see YOU

Sometimes we need a reminder that
God is always with us

Silence The Noise

Silence the noise, Lord
Silence the noise
Every voice that tries to drown out your truth
Every voice that tries to hinder me from reaching my
place
The noise that tries to keep me from seeking your
face

I'm on your path
Not knowing where it leads
I am sustained
Sustained I am
You keep me all the way
Though at times I may stray

It's lonely here
So lonely here
But still I hear you calling for me to come near
Your voice is calling, "I'm over here"

Trust me now
I will never let you down
Keep walking on my path
Keep walking on my path
Everything will become clear as you draw near

Stay In Your Lane

I don't have time to criticize others

I'm too busy asking the Lord to work on me

WORK ON ME JESUS!

Still Anchored

Don't be confused
Don't sugar coat it
Be real
Tell the truth
Don't be ashamed to be honest
Don't make promises you can't back up
Don't keep your head in the sand and live in denial
Don't continue to pray that all the problems will just
go away
Let's be real

Being a Christian does not mean everything will
always go right
It doesn't mean that every day will be bubbly
That's not true
That's not real
Storms will come
That's a promise
Situations happen
Disappointments are a part of life
Pain is a part of life

As a Christian, I would never tell someone their days
of struggle are over
I would never tell them they will never face any
challenges, or tragedy
God uses difficult times to mature us
I think that's the hardest thing for us to believe and
accept

I will tell them that while going through the struggles
in life, their hope can be anchored in Jesus Christ
I will tell them that they are not alone

We learn about ourselves, and we learn about God in
times of testing
We learn about the promises in His Word
We learn how to trust God
It's a process
We learn about Him through our trials

Our faith is strengthened through experiencing trials
We learn how to pray instead of worrying
We learn how to forgive instead of being bitter
We learn how to have courage while trusting and
depending on Jesus Christ

Jesus Christ is our hope
Our only hope
No matter what you face in life, with Jesus Christ, you
can still be anchored

Still Valuable

Remind yourself everyday
That you are still valuable

You may be a little torn
But you are still valuable

No matter what the circumstances

You are not a throw away

You may have made some bad choices
But you are still valuable

You may have believed the lie of the enemy
But you are still valuable

You may have felt like giving up

DON'T!!!

You are still valuable

Suddenly!

God can make it happen SUDDENLY!

Get Ready!

No doubt about it
There's nothing impossible for God
Nothing
He wants only the best for His children
I'm receiving everything God has for me

How about you?

Take Inventory

Have you taken a long look at your baggage lately?
I mean a long, hard look
Not pretty is it?
Nope
How long have you had the stuff?
Have you ever taken inventory?
What are you still holding onto?
Why?
Have you labeled your baggage?
Did you forget you just hid it away somewhere?
Still trying to cover it up
Hoping no one will see it
Don't want to talk about it
Don't want to think about it
Hope it will just go away
It won't
It's still there
It's a reminder you still have something to take care
of
Avoidance will not make it disappear
Let's see what's inside
Anger
Mistrust
Bitterness
Envy
Jealousy
Unforgiveness
Competition
Lust
Lying

Slander
Greed
Wait. Stop right there
This is too much
There's no way I'm carrying all this stuff around
Really?
Have you asked God about it?

Take Me Higher

How Majestic!
How Wonderful!
I'm waiting for that glorious day
Take me higher
Yes higher, Lord

One day I'll fly away
In your presence, there's glory forevermore
For you I hunger and thirst
Fill me up
Let my cup overflow
I want to go
I want to go higher, Lord
Take my higher

I long to see you face to face
Until that day comes
My work is not done
Give me strength to run my race

Tell Me A Story

Tell me a story
I hope it's good news
Something I've never heard before

Tell me a story of how you've overcome
And who won the war

Tell me a story of how it was before
As you gather your thoughts
Don't be afraid to open that door

Tell me a story, from beginning to end
Eager ears are listening
I'll take a seat, my friend

Tell me a story
I need to know
Is this for real, or just a show?

Tell me a story
So that I may see
I need what you have dwelling in me

Tell me a story, what could it be?
What is this gift you have for me?

Jesus Christ is the Way, the Truth, and Life
Salvation is free
He already paid the price

The Assignment

What has God called you to do?

DO THAT

Be faithful to what God has called you to do
Don't be tossed to and fro

Finish your assignment He gave you now, and then
listen for His voice to get the next one

God will give you the courage to soar!

The Gifts

Who doesn't like to receive gifts?
Everyone loves to receive a gift
A gift anytime of the year
Not just for Christmas
Not just for a birthday
Not just for an anniversary
It doesn't matter
Children
Adults
Male
Female
We love it!
It takes an open hand to receive a gift
Doesn't matter what it comes in
Doesn't matter what size it is
A large box may be impressive
It can also be deceiving
Don't be confused
Only one way to reveal the gift
Open the package
You like surprises?
Open the package
Discover what the gift is
Use it
Appreciate it
Enjoy it!
This is in the natural
How much more in the spiritual?
God gives His children gifts
God decides what those gifts are

Be an open vessel just like the open hand to receive
those gifts
Talk to God about those gifts
Discover what the gifts are
Use the gifts for God's glory
Appreciate the gifts
Stay humble
His gifts are fragile
His gifts are like precious jewels
Handle with care
Enjoy the journey!

The Green Light Is On

Don't let anyone
Intimidate you
Belittle you
Put you in a box
Steal your joy
Devalue you
Make you doubt yourself
Make you doubt God's calling on your life

It's time for you to know who you are in Jesus Christ,
and take your rightful place
Don't worry about the naysayers
Don't worry about the backstabbers
Don't worry about the people who don't want to see
you accomplish anything
Your assignments and destiny have already been
approved by God Himself, with the green light for
GO!

The Impact

Don't see the title
The Impact is more important
It's eternal
There are so many things in life we can find ourselves
chasing after
And that would include titles, positions, cliques,
acceptance, affirmation, the ladder of success, etc.
The lists could go on and on

Never let these things be the sole purpose for your
joy, your passion, or feeling you belong
These things alone will never take the place of what is
missing in your spirit and heart
The only person who can fill the emptiness is Jesus
Christ
That's because in all reality we were created for Him
It's all about those things that are eternal

As different people come and go in our lives, we
should always be mindful of the opportunities to
minister life to them
Everyone has a story
Will you be a part of their story?
Will you be the one who leaves an impact in their life?

I want that
I want to hear my Lord and Savior Jesus Christ say to
me, "Well done my good and faithful servant"

The Invitation

Who will take my pain?
You answered
I wandered
You found me
I was held captive
You came
You broke the chains
My path you had written
"Come and Follow Me" you said
Where are we going?
To the other side we'll go
Out of the darkness into
The Light
You are The Light
There is your abode
Revealed The Way
You re The Way
And seeing I shall go
And hearing I shall know
"Come and Follow Me" you said
I am here

The Power Of Words

Bricks and stones break bones
Words will never hurt
YOU LIED!
Words can hurt
You can't see it
It's still here

See this?
Here's the scar
Here's the wound
I'm touched to the core
My heart is in pieces

I don't like myself
What am I worth?
How much did this pain cost you?
Everything!

Was it worth it?
Was the time well spent?
The damage is deep
No one knows how deep

How do I recover?
Lord, help me to recover
I look to you
Make me over

You forgot one thing
Where's your salt?

You left out the salt
The taste is bitter
It's very bitter

Lord, cover me with your grace
Teach me to do better
I want to do better
Make my words a healing balm
Let them hear YOU when I speak

The Promise

Hold on to the promises of the Lord
Hold on to the promises in His Word
For you shall reap
Yes, you shall receive
Hold on to the promises of the Lord
The Lord is faithful
So faithful
He's faithful to complete what He has started
The Lord is faithful
So faithful
To fulfill His promise to you

The Question

Do you hear the cry?
That awful cry
The cry for help
Someone please help

Tell me, do you hear the sound?
That terrible sound
The sound of hurt
The sound of pain

We're in trouble
Lord, we're in trouble
Many are lost in this place
Jesus, we're calling on Your Name

No more pretending we don't see
No more hoping it will go away
It's time to ask yourself what role do I play in making
it better

Father, forgive us
We depend on you
Every day we will seek your face
We need to hear from you

The Unwanted Visitor

There was no phone call
No knock at the door
Nothing spoken
No questions asked
I'm sure nothing was said
No invitation mailed
But still you came

When did you decide you would drop by?
Without my permission you arrived
You decided I didn't need to know
You were mistaken
But still you came

You hid in the corner
No one knew where you were
No one knew you would come
You invaded my life without a clue
How dare you!
The order of things has changed because of you

When I look in the mirror
What do I see?
An unwanted visitor who has taken space in me
Do not be confused
You are not my friend
Your visit here is quickly coming to an end

So as you leave

DONNA R. RUTHERFORD

Let me remind you again
You are not welcome
No vacancy here
A return visit has been cancelled
And I win!

There's Healing In The

Dirt

Sometimes you find your healing in
connecting with people

Find the right people who will be with you
during the process of your journey

You need true friends who don't mind getting dirty

See beyond your pain, so you can see the pain in
others

This Moment

In this moment, I will draw near
I feel your presence
There is no fear

In this moment, I will embrace
Draw me closer
Draw me closer

No words spoken
But I know to come
No thought of what I will see
I feel your presence
I will seek your face
Draw me closer
Draw me closer

In this moment, I will enter in
Such a sweet fragrance draws me near
Your healing touch is everywhere

Oh, the Glory!
Oh, the Glory!
In this place

To My Mighty Sons

THERE IS A KING IN YOU!

Do you know how much you are loved?
I'm so proud of you. I'm so thankful I can call you
my son. It doesn't matter how many times you've
missed the mark. It doesn't matter how many times
you may have made bad decisions, or even failed.
You are still my son. And you are still loved

You are already accepted by the Beloved. There's
nothing more you can do to meet His approval. You
are already accepted. You are His. You've been
marked. You were marked while you were in my
womb. Never forget that. Don't lose your place.
Don't lose your ground. You've already started
walking. Keep walking forward to complete the task.
Be mindful of the company you keep. Don't go to
the left or right. Keep moving forward. Don't be
persuaded to take another path. Your path has
already been established. Your feet are established in
the Lord

Don't listen to the hissing sound of the enemy. He
can be so cunning. And his voice may sound right. It
may make sense. It may seem logical. The Lord's
Word must be discerned by the Spirit. You my son,
know the voice of the Lord. As He has told you
many times, "My sheep know my voice. And another
they will not follow." You will not follow the other
voice. The other voice will lead to destruction

You've come so far. Why change now? Why go another way now? Who has persuaded you? Who has tricked you? Not only that, you are needed. Oh yes, there is a purpose for you being here. You will cause damage to the kingdom of darkness. Yes, you will tread on serpents. You will open your mouth and the Lord's sword will shoot the target. Yes, the aim will be correct. You will not miss, as long as you use the right weapon. The weapon I've given you.

You've always been unsettled. Trying different things. Always looking for something new. Tasting new things. Following the crowd. Still not being satisfied. Not being content. My son, what are you looking for? Is not the Word of God enough? All the answers are in His Word. God's Word has already been established. It's already completed.

It's time to settle down. Shake off the boredom. Shake off the uneasiness. It's time to settle down. THERE IS A KING IN YOU! And He's ready to do business through you.

I will love you always!

Ma

To My Precious

Daughter

Where has the time gone? The years are
just flying by! I remember going into labor
with you. And I'm sure you've heard me say that
more than once

My mind goes back to so many wonderful memories.
Your father use to pick you up and put you on his
shoulders while walking around the block. You loved
it! You were laughing so hard

Do you remember my favorite hairdo for you? Little
hair balls and twists. I would crisscross your twists at
the top of your head with colorful balls and barrettes.
You hated it! I still have that school picture of you,
and you asked me, "Ma, what were you thinking?" I
thought that hairdo was cute! LOL

Oh and I can't forget the many times your father and
I would take you on a long car ride, or pushed you in
your stroller to help you fall asleep. You know what?
It worked! Your father would be talking to you, and
you'd be fast asleep

I remember when you were valedictorian of your
class. We all were so proud of you. You put a lot of
hard work into your grades and studies. You

deserved it

You went through the same peer pressure that most teens encounter, but you learned and grew from it. We had our rough spots and trying period, but we never stopped loving and caring for each other. You're not my little baby anymore. You've matured into a beautiful young woman. You have a heart for caring for people, and you value your friendships

I can sit back and laugh at our conversations of you reminding me you thought I was getting a little forgetful. And I would remind you of what my dad would tell his children: "You just keep on living." Aging happens daughter, if you're blessed to live long enough! LOL

Your journey is all about you finding your place in God's plans for you. Continue to be as beautiful as you are, daughter.

I will love you always!

Ma

Truth

Personal views and opinions
will never, ever change the
Word of God

God's Word is the only thing that will stand forever

TRUTH is what will liberate you. Not someone's
opinion of you

The Word of God is TRUTH. His Word is what I
believe about me

His Word is what I stand on about me

His Word is what I receive about me

Underneath The Wrap

Long Hair
Short Hair
Hair Extensions
Yes
No
Wigs
Straight
Curled
Colored
Can't Decide
Make Up
On
Off
Jewelry
Layered
Bolo
Round-Cut
Pear-Shape
I'll Take It
Dangles
Beads
Movado
Citizen
Chic
Vintage
Designers
Pumps
Stilettos
Corporate
Glass Ceiling

I FEEL LIKE BUSTING LOOSE!
Full-Time
Part-Time
Retired
Profit
Non-Profit
Entrepreneur
Business Owner
Ministry

God, what is my purpose?

At the end of the day, underneath the wrap, who are
you?
Who is the real YOU?
What is your passion?
What is God's plan and purpose for you?

The Wrap covers the outward.
It's time to remove the layers and reveal what is
underneath

What If?

What if …

You have an opportunity to be a sponsor in a life-changing event. Would you?

You were given money to attend college for four years. Your passion is to go to Medical School, which would require more years and money. Would you?

The Lord Jesus Christ commanded you to pray for and forgive your abuser. Would you?

You are ready to step out of your comfort zone, but you're more concerned about what other people think. Would you?

The Lord Jesus Christ reveals to you that He wants to take you to another level in Him. He's requiring you to walk away from all the resources you're holding on to. You've invested time, love and energy into it all. Would you?

We all have been given opportunities over the years for new adventures. Opportunities that would stretch us, change us, and require accountability. For some of us, we desire to do things better, but we're stuck.

We're stuck on the same old way of doing things. We're stuck with the same old crowd we hang around. We're stuck on believing the negative opinions of others. We're stuck on being a people pleaser.

We're stuck with working with friends and family members that don't believe we can progress anyway. We're stuck on staying in our box. We're stuck on staying in our familiar comfort zone. We're stuck on our struggles in our mind. We're stuck on holding a grudge. We're stuck on trying to forgive. We're stuck on fear. We're stuck on taking the necessary steps for healing. We're stuck on trying to believe we can do it.

What if there was a better way of doing things? Different possibilities. Change your view. Change your perspective. Change your environment. Be willing to change. Be willing to grow.

No one can walk the path of life alone. We're not created to be lone rangers. We need one another. There are resources that God has created for us to tap into. Those resources can only be discovered if you learn to reach out to others. Someone else has gifts and talents that you need for your growth, and vice versa.

The Lord Jesus Christ is the source for everything we need. He wants you to find your courage to change and grow. You need to get unstuck, and He is the only one that can help you do it.

What's In A Word?

Words carry a lot of weight

The right words can help lift the burden
The wrongs words can weigh you down

The right words can change your view
The wrong words keep you in a box

The right words can teach you how to love YOU
The wrong words cause you to doubt yourself

The right words help you to see yourself as God does
The wrong words cause you to have low self-esteem

The right words help you to love and forgive
The wrong words cause you to hate and be bitter

The right words help you to live in peace
The wrong words cause strife and anger

The right words help you to believe and walk by faith
The wrong words cause you to live in fear

Choose the RIGHT words

What's Your Name?

The weather forecast for today
Partly sunny
Change of showers
60°
Kinda dreary
Gotta get moving
My back hurts
Here we go again
All is good with the world
I had a dream I was sleeping on clouds
What time is it?
Let me see
What's on my calendar?
Looks like I have room
I'm free today
I think I'll switch socks
Wore the blue ones yesterday
What's that smell?
Coffee
I need some coffee
What's that commotion?
Foot steps
I could use a cigarette right now
Those things can kill ya
Yeah, I know
What's up Joe?
There's that dude
Man, your language sucks
Don't touch me
Oh, I forgot

You don't shake hands
Probably an antibacterial thing
Get a job
Heard that yesterday
Do you always repeat yourself?
Here's another one
I see the glares
Still not use to the stares
What's that smell?
Oh. It's me
Another night
Sleep tight
Time to change my neighborhood
Good morning, world
Maybe today will be better
I had a dream I was eating hotcakes and sausage
Hello
Thought I'd bring you some breakfast
Ask me
Go ahead
Ask me
What's your name?
My name is Donna

Who Told You?

Who told you

You

Are not

ENOUGH?

Don't

Believe

The lie

YES!

Say YES! to the Lord Jesus Christ

YES! to His tugging at your heart

Say YES! to admitting you need Him

Say YES! to an intimate, personal relationship with
Him

YES! to His loving you

YES! to His forgiving you

Say YES! to His changing you

YES! to His plans and purpose for you

Say YES! to His desire to live in your heart

Say YES! to live with Jesus Christ for eternity

You Are A Wonder

O God! O God!
You are a wonder
O Lord how great
How great you are
My God! My God!
You are a wonder
All heaven and earth
Heaven and earth
Shows your glory
My God! My God!
You are a wonder
My God, I worship you
Lord, I worship you
You are a wonder
All honor is due Your Name
Glory is due Your Name
You are a wonder

You Are Enough

I don't want to be like everyone else

You are a blessing just as you are. You were created
in the image of God

There are so many gifts inside of you just waiting for
you to discover them

You don't have to be a copycat of someone else

The Lord's plan for you was designed and created just
for you. Be excited about it!

It's time for you to see yourself as God sees you

YOU ARE ENOUGH!

You Are Glorious!

You are Glorious!
O God, you are Glorious!
You reign in majesty
You have set the captives free with your power and
might
I sing Glory!
I sing Glory!
I give you thanksgiving and praise with a grateful
heart
All glory and honor
Wisdom and power
Belongs to you
There is no one like you
No one like you
Life begins with you
You make all things new

You are Glorious!
O God, you are Glorious!
Just the mention of your Name
Your wonderful Name
Gives me peace beyond words
Joy! Unspeakable Joy!
Greets me in the morning dew
You are the sunshine of my day
And the sweet sleep of my night

You are Glorious!

O God, you are Glorious!
I run to you with arms open wide
You lift me up
In you I can hide
I'm fulfilled
I'm made whole
It's all because of you
You are the lover of my soul

You Get Me

Hello Friend! Hello You! Yes You!
I just wanted to say I really appreciate you. I know
we joke around a lot, and at times don't take each
other seriously, but this time I mean it. I appreciate
you. You see me. You get me. I don't have to put
on airs. I don't have to wear a mask around you. I
don't have to try and impress you. You take me just
as I am. You see me. You get me.

With you, I can speak my mind, and not be ashamed.
We both have said things to each other that was
hurtful. Those words may have been the truth, but
they were still hurtful. We've had some
misunderstandings. Pretty ugly. At the end, we
always would look at each other and realize we didn't
want to lose our best friend. Getting reconciled was
more important than being right. In those moments,
you knew when I was just venting, and needed a hug
from my friend. You see me. You get me.

We've both endured hardship and disappointment
over the years. That's life. One thing I do know, you
are a strong woman. You seem to bounce right back.
It doesn't matter what the circumstances, you light up
the room wherever you go. You always bring enough
smiles to share. You know just the right thing to say.
You are my cheerleader. You see me. You get me.

You are a jewel, and I love you dearly. Thanks for
being my best friend!

About the Author

Donna R. Rutherford is a native of Washington, D.C., and was educated in the D.C. public school system. She was raised in a Christian home by her wonderful parents, who are both deceased, but did not discover the need for a personal relationship with Jesus Christ until an adult. As a child, she was always searching and asking questions. Little did she know, God's hand was on her at an early age, and He would be the only one that could fill the void in her spirit and heart.

As an adult, she received her Associate Degree in Business Administration. She also received a variety of certificates from Evangel Cathedral's Bible School, and School of Leadership, located in Upper Marlboro, Maryland. Her ministries included the Choir, Altar Ministry, and Alms Ministry.

Donna has a heart for serving the needy and homeless. Her desire is to help them get on their feet, so they can see themselves as God sees them. She was also involved with the Hope and Restoration Ministries, an Outreach Ministry for the needy, founded by Apostle Robin Harris. Over the years, she has also written speeches during her participation in

Power Toasters.

She is the founder of *Reconciled to Wholeness Ministries*, a ministry dedicated to encourage everyone to see that their journey is not over – God has written every page of their life – and they should not be afraid to turn the page to see the next chapter.

Donna Rutherford is the author of the book, *The Mask of Many Faces*, which is dedicated to everyone who has experienced the pain of rejection and self-worth. This book is about her story and journey in discovering her true identity in Jesus Christ.

Her second book, *It's Time to Manifest*, is an inspirational book as a reminder of the promises of God to continue to walk in the calling He has placed on a person's life, while pursuing Him.

She is the proud mother of two sons, and one daughter. They continue to be her joy.

She is a motivated author, poet, speaker and lyricist dedicated to giving inspirational and biblical encouragement. Her heart is to see reconciliation and the power of the Word of God changing lives. The Bible continues to be her source of inspiration.